DEDICATION

To all the warriors of the rainbow who have lived before, who flourish now, and will live again—to heal the Earth and the collective soul of her people. You are deeply loved, known, and supported by Galaxies far and wide.

RAINBOW WARRIOR

ACTIVATION DECK GUIDEBOOK

WRITTEN BY
TRACEE DUNBLAZIER

ILLUSTRATED BY
JUSTINE SEREBRIN

GoTracee Publishing LLC
Baton Rouge, Louisiana Los Angeles, California

Copyright ©2018 Tracee Dunblazier, Justine Serebrin

All rights reserved. No part of this book may be used or reproduced in any manner without the written permission of the publisher.

GoTracee Publishing LLC
240 Laurel Street, Suite 101
Baton Rouge, Louisiana, 70801
www.BeASlayer.com

ISBN: 978-0-9963907-5-0

Illustrations and Cover Design: Justine Serebrin
www.earthaltarstudio.com

Interior Design: Divya Jyoti Darpan www.mahaketudesign.com

Editing: Stephen J. Miller www.thekeepersofmanaan.com

Disclaimer: The Rainbow Warrior Activation Deck and Guidebook set is for entertainment purposes only. No information and opinions offered through this title, through GoTracee Publishing LLC., or through any other venue representing Tracee Dunblazier or Justine Serebrin are to be substituted for appropriate mental health or medical help. In no event are Tracee Dunblazier or Justine Serebrin, their agents and/or representatives liable for any damages whatsoever arising out of or in any way connected with any individual's interpretation or use of information contained in this title. By reading this title you recognize and agree to take complete and total responsibility for yourself, your experience, and your actions.

Printed in China

ACKNOWLEDGEMENTS

I'd like to thank my tribe in the sky and Mama Wiea, my tribe on Earth and at Earth Altars Studio, and everyone who has supported me and contributed to fulfilling my vision. A special thank-you to Tracee for activating this deck into completion and published bliss. Know that I am forever grateful.

With Love,
Justine Serebrin

TABLE OF CONTENTS

Dedication	iii
Acknowledgements	v
Introduction	ix
How to Use the Cards	xi
Can I use these cards to do readings for others?	xii
Preparation for Choosing the Cards	xii
Interpreting the Cards	xii
Storing the Cards	xiii
Methods of Reading	xiv
Reading Spreads	xiv

1	Action	3
2	Activation	5
3	Air	7
4	Alchemy	9
5	Allow	11
6	Ancestors	13
7	Animal Spirits	15
8	Autumn	17
9	Child	19
10	Crown Chakra	21
11	Crystal Spirits	23
12	Darkness	25
13	Divine Intelligence	27
14	Early Summer	29
15	Earth Element	31
16	Explorer	33
17	Father Sky	35
18	Fire	37
19	Forgiveness	39
20	Freedom	41

Table of Contents

21	Galactic Portal	43
22	Great Mother	45
23	Grounding	47
24	Guardian	49
25	Healer	51
26	Healing Field	53
27	Heart Chakra	55
28	Intention	57
29	Late Summer	59
30	Leap	61
31	Life Force	63
32	Mastery	65
33	Matrix	67
34	Metal	69
35	Music	71
36	Plant Medicine	73
37	Radiance	75
38	Release	77
39	Root	79
40	Sacral Chakra	81
41	Shadow	83
42	Shaman	85
43	Solar Plexus	87
44	Spring	89
45	Synergy	91
46	Third Eye	93
47	Throat Chakra	95
48	Union	97
49	Visionary	99
50	Warrior	101
51	Water	103
52	Winter	105

INTRODUCTION

You have all the answers. Feeling overwhelmed is a natural part of the spiritual process of change. Learning to cultivate your intuition and access the information you need when you can most use it, is a skill. One that can easily be thwarted by developments that happen around you every day, for which you have no control.

Feeling powerless, on any level, is the number one contributor to making regretful decisions.

The only real solution for addressing the divergent forces in today's world is by unifying the ones in your heart and mind. It only takes a small adjustment of focus to shift a perspective of powerlessness to one that can change your life for the better right now.

Cultivating self-trust is the key.

That's why intuitive artist Justine Serebrin and renowned spiritual empath Tracee Dunblazier teamed up to create the RAINBOW WARRIOR ACTIVATION DECK. It's exactly the tool you need to embrace your own heart-opening spiritual unification process and activate your deepest soul knowledge.

It's true: everything you need, you have. It's imprinted in your spirit. The quantum shift from living unconsciously—at your soul's beck and call—to surrendering yourself to an amplified awareness is profound. Using the RAINBOW WARRIOR ACTIVATION DECK can make your transition easy and fun.

As the magnetic field of our planet changes, so does everything on her—including us. Across the globe, extreme immediate transformations are being experienced—from changing friends, family, and community to shifting beliefs, perspective, and ideology. Sometimes, these transitions feel immediate and without warning.

Introduction

Without a doubt, no matter how things appear, you're equipped (on all levels) to master the world—the one around you and the one you've created for yourself—by using the powers that are your birthright. The RAINBOW WARRIOR ACTIVATION DECK can help you—in a conscious way—activate and focus the spiritual knowledge, gifts, and insight you brought into this life. It's what you're being called on to do—now more than ever!

HOW TO USE THE CARDS

The RAINBOW WARRIOR ACTIVATION DECK is a set of transformational art pieces channeled from a council of tribal ancestors with the deep intent to activate and unify human consciousness on this planet. The cards do this by connecting each individual to an awareness of their body, emotions, heart, mind, energy, and soul—done in the very specific language of their superconscious.

The organization of the deck is deliberate; each card uses only a number for identification. This allows you to receive and mirror back your own spiritual images and understanding as they are inspired by your unique perception of the art. The images will trigger transformational archetypes while the guidebook offers a set of varied options expressing the profound energetic dynamics that are occurring in your life. As you expand your awareness, your deck and its cards' meanings will grow with you.

During your reading, it's important to take a moment of quiet with each card to allow the activation and mirroring process. Take notes, if you'd like, of the thoughts and images that come to mind; follow where they lead. Then, consult the RAINBOW WARRIOR ACTIVATION DECK guidebook. It will give you a set of diverse meanings, offering you the opportunity to identify your first instinct while intuiting the current meaning and the application thereof to your present circumstances or situation.

Your intuitive development moves in a sacred pattern, leading from your own personal imprints and truth to the shared universal Truth; the meaning of each card will follow this pattern as well. As one develops their perspective, the card meanings and visual art will transition too—so be prepared to open to new insights every day.

Introduction

CAN I USE THESE CARDS TO DO READINGS FOR OTHERS?

For the novice: Of course you can, with one caveat. Often when reading for others, whether personally or professionally, you'll attract folks with whom you share a common ground. Dive in, embracing the idea that the information coming through for them also applies to you. While you may not share similar perspectives or experiences as your querent, you may find alignment in the spiritual dynamic at play.

For the professional: You'll enjoy the inspired activation that the images of this deck will promote in your readings—connecting you to new perspectives, languages, and expanded interpretations of archetypal dynamics. The beautifully ambiguous and richly colorful images naturally elevate you and your clients out of any form of emotional resistance that might result from the *fear of knowing* or the weariness of compassion-fatigue that often comes with the job of counseling others.

PREPARATION FOR CHOOSING THE CARDS

You can use this deck any way you want: on the fly, for lengthier meditative sessions, for readings with others, or however it serves you best. In each case, take a moment to breathe deep and let relaxation wash over you. If you'd like the cards to inspire you—clear your mind and pull as many cards as you want. When you're wanting specific information—center that question in your mind and heart, or visualize the experience or circumstance for which you seek guidance, before pulling the cards.

INTERPRETING THE CARDS

The cards and their connotations are intended to trigger your deep archetypal resonance, and to ground in higher spiritual wisdom—and fuller insight—of the subjects at hand, beginning with your own language. Every individual will relate to these cards differently as they move through unique experiences, cycles, and perspectives. The RAINBOW WARRIOR ACTIVATION DECK will expand in significance as your own spiritual activation and integration evolves.

STORING THE CARDS

You and your process are sacred; the cards are paper and can be replaced. That said, your RAINBOW WARRIOR ACTIVATION DECK, while magnificently beautiful, is definitely sturdy and can take a lot of use. Still, you might want to keep your cards stored in their box. For ritual purposes, wrap the box in your favorite reading cloth or scarf, or keep stored in your medicine bag. The practice of unwrapping will naturally become the action that triggers deep breathing and relaxation as you begin your descent into illumination.

METHODS OF READING

Traditional spiritual card or tarot reading requires following a protocol—not so with the RAINBOW WARRIOR ACTIVATION DECK. Any way you choose to use the deck is spirit's way of helping you access the biggest value for you. However, the use of a reading ritual is helpful in organizing, grounding, and expressing new information, and we highly support your own creation of one.

Here are some options for you to consider:

- Serve yourself a sacred beverage of your choice
- Light a candle
- Take four deep breaths
- Unwrap the deck
- Shuffle the deck
- Cut the deck in half or thirds
- Focus on the question at hand, or clear your mind and heart to receive the message
- Do a happy dance
- Choose your cards
- Splay the deck in front of you; or choose from the top; or while shuffling, see which cards fall out or make themselves known to you
- When your reading for the day is complete, rewrap your deck and say a prayer of gratitude

READING SPREADS

Theme of the Day/Week

Life is a series of spiritual patterns that connect us to all things. Use this type of reading to lock on to the active pattern expressing itself in your day and how you can amplify or adjust its flow.

Introduction

Choose one to three cards for your theme of the day or at the beginning of your week. Glean from them the spiritual and energetic dynamics at work in your life during this time. As you go through your day, more information will reveal itself to you. At days end, reflect on your theme and how its wisdom applies to your circumstances or experiences of the day.

Daily Spiritual Insight

Pull a single morning card for insight to consider throughout your day, or a nightly card to focus your dreamtime on illuminating you to your deeper realities, possibilities, and joys to come.

MORNING CARD

Three Card Reading

A three card reading can be read from left to right—past, present, and future. It's best used to tell the story of how you became engaged in your current life situation and how to best complete or expand it.

PAST   PRESENT   FUTURE

Introduction

Five Card Reading

A five card reading can be read left to right as a story board or in a traditional cross form with a card in the middle representing you.

Story Board Reading

Celtic Cross Reading

- Top: the future
- Center: you or the situation
- Left: what you really want or need
- Right: how to access or create it
- Bottom: the past

1

Transition, Response, Energy, Joy, Mindful, Awareness

Action is the transition from one experience to another. The state of motion requires immense presence and awareness. Do you find yourself reacting to things or responding to them? The difference consists of what you know about the events leading up to the current moment, as well as your personal mastery of the circumstances at hand. Biology and habit can often be the impetus for our reactions, but it's our spiritual awareness and choices that will ultimately train the mind and body to respond.

Any action taken now will change your position; pay attention to your environment, feelings, and thoughts. Once you become clear about the move to be made, do it with all the awareness, energy, and joy you can muster. You will meet with the support you need on every level. Breathe—Assess—Focus—Know—GO!

2

Stimulate, Amplify, Trigger, Convert, Willingness, Stasis, Quantum Shift, Sacred Geometry

What is the most prevalent energy active in your life today? Are you ready for a change? Activation heralds a time of Kundalini movement in the body and great change in your perception. Throughout your life since childhood your Chi energy has moved through your body to activate your endocrine system. Each glandular activation is directly related to the spiritual and emotional elements that the particular gland governs.

The activations we are most aware of take place in the fight-or-flight glands of the pancreas (Islets of Langerhans) and the pituitary gland activated at puberty. These activations can cause major shifts in the central nervous system and the chemistry of the body—in addition to how we perceive, think, and feel.

Embrace each awakening; know you are safe by nurturing yourself with love, understanding, patience, and nutrition.

3

Thoughts, Communion, Necessity, Willfulness, Charisma, Demeanor

Air is our presence that is active at all times—it transmits to anyone we come in contact with, and is all-pervasive, complete, and necessary. It is mandatory for life but absent of feeling, so air also represents our mental faculties—our thoughts and ideology.

When Air arrives in your cards, you're being asked to break down your situation to its most basic properties. What do you need and why? Most of all, what message is it sending to others with whom you come in contact? Are you naturally enlisting the support or the repulsion of others?

Allow yourself to become aware of your ever-flowing thoughts and recognize they're as powerful and valuable as air.

4

Chemistry, Partnership, Fusion, Magic, Transmutation, Miracles

Alchemy is the ancient belief that one can turn base metals into gold or, perhaps, find an elixir of everlasting youth.

In other words, it is the creation of a miracle containing the perfect combination of ingredients.

Nowadays, you don't have to go far to find gold—even the Earth's core has enough gold to cover its entire surface. Miracles, on the other hand, we recognize as a series of events—or a process—that we may not have been privy to otherwise (prior to witnessing the fantastic end result).

Know that what you have in your life right now is the making of a miracle, and there is a broader dynamic at work that may not be possible to see from where you're standing. Stay present, and know all is well.

5

Flow, Receptivity, Surrender, Vulnerability, Strength, Expectation

Vulnerability is power at its core; do not consider that it is weakness in any way. To be open to others and the universe takes mastery. Allowing the road to rise up and meet you on your journey is the goal. So if vulnerability and receptivity is a position of power, why do we allow bad things to happen to ourselves, or for others to treat us poorly? How is this a position of strength?

Finding that answer is key to making extraordinary change at this time. When you understand the empowering aspect of your position the changes needed become clear. If the experience is unsavory, do not flinch or move away. Delve in and extract the purpose so you may leave the rest behind. Surrender to the process of receiving everything you need, easily and effortlessly.

6

History, Culture, DNA, Transformation, Spiritual Family, Habits, Tradition

Over the millennia, billions of human beings and other creatures have lived on planet Earth and have left their legacy, whether it be through DNA, transformative events, traditions, or spirit. Understanding what came before you will assist in your current situation, either to clarify what traditions may need to be retired or to point to the strengths and support you are endowed with through your ancestral line.

Respecting your elders and honoring what came before you isn't condoning the erroneous ways of the past—it is embracing the teachings and wisdom they leave behind. Know that your spiritual family surrounds you with love, strength, support, and innovative resolutions to all your life's challenges.

7

Revelation, Support, Ancient Knowledge, Ally, Eternal Love, Directness

Our animal brothers and sisters are powerful allies. They reveal themselves to you in important times of change to offer their wisdom, love, and support. Animals are beautiful in their straightforward simplicity; they are direct and guileless in all of their affairs. They eat when they are hungry, defend themselves when attacked, and are always full of adoration.

If an animal crosses your path in a thought, dream, or the real world it is bringing a message to you from your Creator. Pay close attention. The four-legged or winged ones are conduits of love. They are here to show you how love is expressing itself in your current situation. Look to the traits of the animal spirit at hand to decipher the message.

8

Enjoyment, Restoration, Completion, Wisdom, Experience, Gratitude, Contentment

The autumn portion of the yearly cycle invites you to put down the hammer and nail; relax for a minute and enjoy what you've built. It's a time to harvest gratitude for yourself and others, and to revel in your accomplishments. No need to put any focus on strategizing for the cycle to come… just be present in all you have, and find contentment.

Allowing yourself to settle and surrender to doing nothing is a learned skill. This card is a friendly reminder that being content with what you have doesn't mean you won't have more. It's the time to embrace the fullness of what you've created so that you may generate more from your new standard of wholeness.

9

Innocence, Openness, Folly, Beginning, Growth, Playfulness

We might be under the illusion that children are born a blank slate. The truth is we all enter this world with imprints and soul memories. Childhood is the process of bringing to life this information in a new way. Rediscovering what your spirit knows with a new perspective, wisdom, or inspiration offers you the opportunity to reclaim and transform your soul in the present.

What about your current situation can be viewed with a new lens? Where have you been naive? Where have you given an undeserved benefit-of-the-doubt without doing your research? The process of forgiveness and becoming neutral begins with opening your heart to complete understanding from all vantage points.

10

Inspiration, Access Point, Elevation, Opportunity, Bliss, Link

The more information you have in any situation can be the difference between joy and grief, being alone or lonely, power or force, and knowledge or wisdom. You are being asked to reserve action and carefully evaluate your judgment right now. Things are not exactly as they seem and an expanded awareness is necessary.

At any point within an experience or situation you can stop and take a moment for yourself to be mindful of what you're feeling and access your inner wisdom. Take time to visualize the outcome you want—asking your expanded self if it's the absolute best outcome for you at this time—and then notice your emotions and your body's response to it.

Do you feel conflicted in any way? If so, focusing on resolving that is the next step.

11

Healing, Transmitter, Vibrational Wisdom,
Allowing, Alignment,
Access to Other Realms

The essence of the Universe combined with the compression and nurturing of Mother Earth (for thousands of years) is what every crystal or mineral contains. Sacred geometric forms are the building blocks of many of the crystalline structures—the ancient wisdom born of the trial and error that has come before us.

Each of them communicates their specific message telepathically to whoever is available to receive it. Every crystal and mineral aligns with the vibration of specific mental, emotional, or spiritual dynamics that have been sent here to help humanity heal.

Receiving this card is an indication that the energy of the Crystal Spirits is calling you to heal as well, or to develop a deeper understanding of your experience right now. Working with crystal energy is like defragmenting your computer—reorganizing all the files so you're better able to focus, function, heal, and live more fully.

12

Balance, Duality, Transition, Teacher,
Transformation, Void, Density,
Unconscious

The darkness showed him the ways his life had not been his own. All this time she'd been doing the secret bidding of the dark angel—unaware of the creeping impact on her view. When you are unaware of the unconscious spiritual patterns that drive you, ultimately, they will change the circumstances of your life. At times you are looking for light in a dark place—at others, you are the light in a dark place.

At the end of every cycle there is a transition to a new beginning. It is the most dangerous time in the course of events, and should be respected with reverence and caution. Sometimes it is filled with depression, anxiety, and apathy. Feeling disconnected and careless, even for a time, holds great power and requires immense discipline.

Restless disregard—which may arise from having been freed of ties and obligations belonging to the previous phase—can easily cause you to miss the gems that will prepare you for the cycle ahead. The good news? You are assured that darkness always gives way to light, and there will be a time to move forward again.

13

Co-creation, Love, Purity, Power, Protocol, Confidence, Recognition

All life is manifest from the Divine Intelligence or the vibrational building blocks that created it. Being human, it's easy to forget that the responsibility for creation isn't solely on our shoulders or that we're not subject to the will of an all-seeing force of life.

The Divine Intelligence card is a reminder that we are physical, mental, emotional, spiritual, and energetic manifestations of life's beauty—co-creators of the divine building blocks of love. This card aims to reinforce your confidence.

It also brings your attention to the Universal Truth at play in the current situation: the divine protocol you're being asked to follow—through your heightened awareness at this time—and the complete support you have from your spiritual family, seen and unseen.

14

Activity, Work, Fruition, Stress, Limits, Discipline, Growth, Fear

After spring comes a powerful portion of the yearly cycle—all your hard work comes to fruition. A unique set of principles govern this phase since it is the time before the end of a growing period. Much attention and caution should be paid so that you don't overextend yourself to the point of overload. Don't become complacent or overconfident that the job is done when there might be vital components to finish.

How can setting limits or augmenting discipline bring you over the finish line? Also, understand that fear is a component deeply connected with this moment as well. Something profound is getting ready to be revealed: your bountiful creativity and your numerous accomplishments.

15

Nurture, Nature, Growth, Stability, Commitment, Fundamental, Relationship, Family

The element of earth is comprised of how we plant, nurture, and watch our seeds grow. It is the cool depth of perception we cultivate to support our desires and choices. The earth contains many properties: metals (of all kinds), minerals, and water. The perfect combination of ingredients—in the right measure—is the foundation of growth.

At the moment, what is burgeoning in your life? Is it happiness, a project, a relationship, personal wealth, or fulfilling the needs of others? Take stock of the ingredients you possess and the ones you need in order to realize your creation (try different combinations to see what works best). Don't worry about wasting time; it's best spent honoring what you have, and collecting or cultivating what you don't.

16

Investigation, Expansion, Frivolity, Lightheartedness, Courage, Travel, Comparison, Trust

At some point, during the course of a cycle, exploration of new options is valuable or necessary; albeit, sometimes it's frivolous. Frustration in the face of a stalemate can promote the need to try new things, especially when the old ones have outlived their usefulness.

Practicing new belief systems that create greater opportunity—but may require stronger discipline—is truly an art. Detachment (or becoming present to the wonders of every moment) is the greatest gift to the explorer. This is the time to let go of the tight hold you have on the current situation—in thought or in deed.

There are inherent elements to this process: maintain trust to stay committed to your agreements, identify purpose to investigate new options, and seek inspiration to endure until the cycle is completed. How can you expand your horizons while staying dedicated to your current goals?

17

Promotion, Foundation, Movement, Support, Presence, Generosity, Access, Activation

The all-encompassing never-ending generosity of Father Sky is the energy of support for all life. Accessing this energy and focusing it into your thoughts, desires, and choices will render powerful results at this time. Father serves as a reminder that what we need is always there—even when it's not obvious to us. We are never alone or stuck in one place.

The consistency and stability you bring to your situation is beginning to show. Now is the time to call on the energy of Father Sky to promote your perspective, enhance your vitality, and streamline your focus to the result you're seeking. All is well.

18

Transformation, Passion, Temporal, Preparation, Transition, Innovation

Fire is the great transformer of life; it prepares us for the future. It can remove obstacles and shed light. Sometimes it's the Inspiration we need to make changes quickly in order to receive what we have been preparing for. The Fire element must be nurtured in order to be sustained.

As with Fire, this card augurs that any changes happening now will be completed quickly. Look at what passions you're willing to let go or which ones must be nurtured. Now is the time to surrender to the changes happening; allow the fire to burn away any fears or doubts you may have.

19

Neutrality, Zero Point, Release, Completion, Mercy, Grace, Gratitude

Forgiveness is the final stage of any conflict. It's something you give yourself that will benefit everyone. When we forgive someone (including ourselves) for a transgression, it's not a commitment to forget the transgression; it's a willingness to release yourself from the bitterness or the anger that keeps you attached to the impact of it.

It allows for a return to a wiser and stronger spirit of the self. To achieve grace, you must deconstruct the process that led to what you're experiencing, and then forgive yourself and all others from that zero point. Another idea of forgiveness is gratitude.

The recognition of the gains made from any obstacle in your path. Being thankful, not for the betrayal-at-hand, but for your fortitude in overcoming it and the confidence that now wells up inside of you.

20

Rebel, Choice, Awareness, Rejoice, Movement, Enslavement, Release

Freedom is a way of life we choose for ourselves or offer to another. World history is littered with instances of the enslavement of people or the subjugation of ideas, as well as the stealing away of possibility or the denial of opportunity. Ultimately, however, we are charged with the responsibility of releasing ourselves from the bondage by which we are imprisoned.

Attachment is a powerful dynamic we use to learn cooperation with the outer world; *detachment* teaches independence of the inner world. True freedom, however, comes from transcending both: embracing a position defined by the complete acceptance of—and the total surrender to—the circumstances at hand.

This spiritual concept may feel a lot like apathy, but in truth, it is the purist form of love and compassion. From what do you need to free yourself? How can you live in freedom?

21

Cosmos, Transcendence, Extra-Terrestrial, Deep Understanding, Clairsentience, Knowing, Belief, Art

Some people believe that there are things beyond our human comprehension. What do you believe? We may not have the words to describe what we know, but it doesn't mean we don't know it. Tapping into our deep understanding to trust what our heart tells us to be true, even without physical proof.

Begin the work of trust by channeling through and giving expression to the impressions you experience through any modality you choose. This card is asking you to trust your inner universal knowing—not your fear, anger, ignorance, or confusion.

Take a deep breath and ask yourself what is true in your current situation?

22

Source, Foundation, Secure, Sustain, Balance, Generosity, Unconditional Love

Great Mother is the life force that sustains us all. Her ecosystem is the greatest teacher regarding the interconnectedness of all things and the impact they have on one another, without fail. Mother Earth doesn't pick and choose who she supports with all her resources; therefore, her ability to safeguard her own existence and rebalance what humans have made uneven is relentless and can appear unmerciful.

Are you giving generously from your supply of resources? Or are you pushing others' boundaries to the point where radical steps are needed to achieve equity? Receiving this card heralds a time when balance is paramount. Recognize the cost of the people, the places, and the things in your life—and your cost to them.

23

Depth, Center, Clarity, Focus, Comfort, Knowing, Connection

The subtle ebbs and flows of life are the building blocks of your experiences. Your ability to relax and concentrate allows you to receive and use new information. Grounding is the dynamic of connection and the use of the newly retrieved data. Centering yourself creates a feeling of comfort and familiarity that leads to a state of relaxation and receptivity.

What is new about this information for you? Delve deeper into your circumstances or needs to better understand why they exist—this will be the key to your success right now.

A grounding ritual: take four deep breaths and visualize a cord of light from the Creator flowing down through the top of your head, down your spine, and through the bottom of your feet to the golden core of the earth.

24

Spirit Guide, Protection, Sanctuary, Preservation, Conservation, Salvation, Belief

In the real world (and all the other dimensions), there are many conditions that inspire different forms of guardianship: peace in a time of confusion, conservation in a time of drought, spirit guides teaching and protecting us on all levels, or forgiveness and mercy when our hearts are breaking.

No matter the type of protection, we will traverse both sides of these relationships during our tenure on the planet. Is there someone you need to forgive, or offer your voice to when theirs is jumbled and confused? What beliefs or ideals do you hold that no longer serve and support you?

Now is the time to take an in depth look at who and what protects you, and why. Is your protection of another enabling them to grow or not? Take this opportunity to share your gratitude with all who champion your well being.

HEALER

25

Empath, Juxtaposition, Deep Feeling, Embrace, Fortitude, Transmutation

Understanding is the great healer, and empathy teaches us to understand. Healing traditions all around the globe practice the art of reconnection—to the Creator, to ourselves, or to others. In reality, we are never actually disconnected. The idea of this division, in all the ways it may appear to you, is an illusion to be repaired or transitioned.

How can you look at the subject at hand from a new vantage point? Cultivating your empathy by tuning in and asking to feel what another feels can transcend words. It creates a bridge and a bond that strengthens everyone. You are a healer—what do you need to heal?

26

Relaxation, Epigenome, Honesty, Resonance, Healing, Space, Balance

Research has proven that when we're feeling relaxed, secure, and comfortable, our DNA is relaxed too. Relaxed DNA will find ways to heal itself, or adapt and change to cause health. On an energy level, we call this the healing field.

It is the energetic signature we can focus on to create a balancing of our mind, body, and spirit. In the physical body, it is the role of the Epigenome that causes the necessary transformations. Make no mistake about it, healing requires change on every level.

In fact, by the time we experience disease in the physical realm, we've been struggling with imbalance in all of the other dimensions for quite some time. The good news here is that any change on any plane of existence will ignite the healing process for all of them. Get on board!

27

Compassion, Love, Fullness, Emptiness, Generosity, Eternity, Adoration

The heart is the crossroads between our human body and the Creator. The first organ to manifest in a human embryo is the heart, from which the tongue grows. Every word we speak—or kiss we give—is an expression of our divine power in the physical world, and it is wise to treat it as such.

Expanding your view of the current experience or situation to a more heartful place can have a profound impact on the timing and expediency needed to transform what's inside or outside of you. Crying tears of truth releases what no longer suits you, creating a space for what is now needed. You are eternally adored—every part, always.

28

Foundation, Create, Concentrate, Attract, Belief, projection, Blueprint

Intention is the foundation of an idea being called into manifestation. It creates an energetic blueprint, including the idea to be fulfilled and everything needed to bring the idea into completion (mentally, emotionally, physically, and spiritually). There is purpose in all things, so it's important to take heart in your current situation.

Consider the foundation you are sitting upon and exactly what intention created it. What need has already been met? What need has it left you with? Our intentions often stem from a limited view of our situation. If that's the case, you may want to elevate your intention to a less limited concept like *happiness*, *fulfillment*, *stability*, or an *easy flow*. Leave the creative judgment to your higher realms.

29

Fruition, Manifestation, Harvest, Fullness, Reward, Results, Obviousness

Late summer is a time of harvest and the evidence of hard work becoming manifest. It is the point in any cycle where achievement is imminent and the slow decent to a new beginning commences. Now is the time to begin clearing the slate of unfinished projects, no-longer-needed items, and unspoken sentiment.

Receiving this message in your cards lets you know that what you are experiencing now is a result of your previous focus and direction—good, bad, or indifferent. It's the universal response to your efforts. Celebration is always called for here, as what can be seen in its physical form can be changed, modified, or amplified; and thusly, a new cycle begins.

30

Motivate, Plunge, Depth, Overwhelm, Congruency, Tap, Faith

The only thing that keeps you from success is quitting. To accomplish anything, it is often a long sequence of multiple elements coming together. Ebbs and flows are a part of the process. Don't let having advance knowledge of them intimidate you. Quite a bit goes into enduring through a project or cycle of growth to its completion; there is a time for equilibrium and a time for rapid movement.

Leaping further into yourself or your situation will bring about ultimate success. Any illumination you receive from this deep dive—whether good, bad, or indifferent—is ultimately better to have, and it's crucial to move forward. Do not lose sight of your fortitude, strength, and integrity. Jump!

31

Kundalini, Union, Merkabah, Activation, Opening, Network

Who you are is a result of Divine Intelligence activating the life force energy, or Kundalini, in your body. The combined forces create a powerhouse able to transform all frequencies of your spiritual, mental, emotional, and physical bodies. Based on how we think, feel, nurture, and receive universal light energy, science is now proving that our DNA is able to change, heal, and adapt as necessary.

This ever-growing evolutionary birthright is at work in your own life today. Allow yourself to surrender to a fuller awareness of your body (on all levels) and how it functions. Pay attention to any imbalances; look for their original causes so you may find resolution and regain your equilibrium.

32

Acceptance, Completion, Level Up, Expansion, Accountability, Confidence, Meticulous

Mastery is fully accepting the way things are and being accountable for them. To become masterful, then, is to embrace the situation or experience as it is, so you may begin the work of changing your role or leveling up. You don't need to know everything in order to have mastery, and needn't have shame about the things you don't know.

Most importantly, you must have a willingness to go towards your situation and access all you need, with a spirit of motivation and aptitude. You're being called upon to let go of worry and panic. Accept that you know exactly what is happening and are aware of every detail—believe that you now have the confidence to change or to complete something in a powerful way.

33

Etheric Layer, Aura, Organization, Order, Eternity, Patterns

All things transmit an energetic signature we receive and interpret, long before the experience becomes physical (when we're able to see, hear, or taste what's happening). It is because of this patterning that we experience repetition. Repetition, of course, is how we learn things—by experiencing them over and over again. It takes at least five exposures to new information to hear it for the first time, and many usages of that information to create a habit or memory.

In the matrix of life there are limitless opportunities to create new plot points. Every thought we have creates a new dimension that attracts more ways of expressing its vibration. Are you aware of your thoughts and the feelings that follow them—or of the patterns that generate it all? This card is telling you it's time to pay attention to the subtlety of those patterns and what they are creating in your life.

34

Sharpness, Clarity, Mindfulness, Focused, Determination, Getting the Job Done

Metal is multifaceted—it has many expressions in the physical world. Gold, for example, can be found in almost everything: from the center of the Earth to the bottom of the ocean, and from a eucalyptus leaf to the blood running in your veins. So when someone tells you're made of gold, you really are.

Metal, on an energetic level, refers to your spiritual, emotional, and intellectual integrity. It also represents your ability to be mindful, focused, and clear. Receiving this card today encourages you to work with all aspects of metal energy and to always look for the silver lining.

35

Flow, Harmony, Application, Numbers, Rhythm, Relaxation

Everything in our universe has a numerical relationship (or value), and music is the spiritual understanding of that truth. Every genre of music expresses a vibration—of relaxation, rigidity, or rhythm—and creates a specific flow of movement. It is that eternal movement that weaves together all aspects of life and expression.

Whether the notes are played singularly or in combination, the sounds they create reverberate and change their atmosphere. In your current situation, are you the music or are you being impacted by it? Is the rhythm choppy or smooth, and how are you contributing to it? Turning to the music you are most attracted to at this time, can answer many questions.

36

Origins, Medicine, Structure, Redefine, Messages, Adapt, Interconnectedness

The spirit of our world's history is encapsulated in every seed, stem, and leaf growing on mother Earth. They are the silent witnesses to the evolution and the growth of everything on the planet. From drought and famine to abundance and overgrowth, plant medicine holds the secrets to balancing the mind, body, and spirit—healing all life.

When you are feeling disconnected, call on nature's Divas and Elementals. No beings know more about the importance of honoring the interconnectedness of all things than the trees, the plants, and their guardians. A deep understanding of forest root-systems teach us how family roots keep us safe in times of imbalance.

The ability to survive and adapt is also a part of plant medicine. Receiving this message in your cards today lets you know you are a valuable root in the forest: you provide oxygen to your community, and what you receive is just as significant as what you give.

37

Enjoyment, Fulfillment, Overflow, Firmness, Influence, Expansion, Transmission

Radiance is the constant eternal flow of light that is our birthright. Who we are emanates outward from the light within our being, in spite of personal struggles. Recognizing the beauty of our influence in the world is paramount to our balance and wellbeing.

No matter the state of affairs today, focus on your radiance and the radiance of others. Allow yourself to be open to the overflow of love everywhere you look. Finding fulfillment while loving others is a skill set that must be cultivated—it takes practice. It's different than feeling love. It's about choosing to perceive the adoration that exists all around you. When the Radiance card has chosen you, you're being asked to witness love in all its forms.

38

Completion, Neutrality, Shift, Alter, Boundary, Void, Receive

If you're going to do something at all, you might as well do it right the first time—definitely a philosophy we've all heard once or twice. There is nothing truer than when making efforts to let go of something you no longer need or want in your life. The idea of release is less about getting rid of something and more about changing your relationship to it. (It's true, we release physical things—but unless we change our relationship to them, we'll draw them back in another form.)

Letting go, then, is akin to refocusing your energy in another direction. To be able to do that, you'll need the information and understanding required to complete the process of release: comprehending why you had something in the first place; honoring its memory and grieving its loss; and finally, adjusting your attention to something that better serves your current needs.

Root Chakra

39

Origins, Foundation, Grounding, Basics, Point of Connection

Back to basics is the message of the Root Chakra card. While the Root Chakra of the human energy system governs our most basic needs (such as food, water, rest, and shelter), this card asks you to travel back in time and space to the events that began your current experience. It is the place to bear witness to the original circumstances of your situation and be mindful of their impact on you up until this moment.

At this time, finding forgiveness for yourself and others will allow you to level up from experiences created from need to experiences created from belonging, empowerment, and love.

40

Emotions, Delusion, Creativity, Strain, Filter, Extraordinary Effort, Passion

Emotions and sexual energy are our biggest teachers. Learning the subtlety of their power and using it in love and wisdom is the flow of your current evolution. Any intense energy we experience such as love, anger, or grief is the carrier of a new message from your spirit to your body.

Recognize that what might appear to be negative is really a positive message in its most obscure form. When you focus on the message, the lighter the experience becomes. This is your opportunity to challenge the meaning of the things you feel. If you feel sad, does it mean something bad is happening? Not necessarily. When we express emotion it changes the brain: it clears the way for new energy and a deeper understanding to enter.

41

Underworld, Density, Richness, Foundation, Void, Dispersion, Unconscious

The Shadow is what generates our thoughts, feelings, and choices in the times we lack self-awareness. It is our unconscious self, our spiritual imprints, and the place where all our soul memories are stored. The Shadow is our greatest source of power, and fear can be a mechanism that will bring you to full awareness of a given moment.

Proceed boldly; get all the information about your current situation. Do not fear what will come to pass. Examine what is generating your fear and change it within yourself, thereby eliminating your fear altogether. Be present. Breathe through the adrenaline and know you are safe. Being able to see the entire situation allows for decisive movement and thorough follow through.

42

Spiritual Journey, Soul Retrieval, Perseverance, Illusion, Success

The Shaman's journey is one of courage and faith on all levels: traveling on behalf of another to the root of an experience that is revealing its discordant presence in the subject's mind, body, or spirit. Being of service this way is a powerful testament to the Shaman's endurance through long-suffering: they are able to bear witness to another's pain without judgment and with compassion.

This card is evidence that you possess this skill set, are working to cultivate it, or are in need of it. During this stage of spiritual development you will experience Kundalini energy movement, lucid/vivid dreams, intuitive clairvoyant visions, and deeper empathy for yourself and others. Understand, it is futile to resist the flow of this process! Breathing deeply and surrendering to it will be the wise course.

43

Power, Presentation, Position, Concoct, Implementation, Fabricate, Presence

Nothing is more valuable in terms of human interaction than first impressions—or how you present your position. Regardless of its truth, others will remember what you say about yourself; they'll remember your disposition or the confidence of your actions, even if you don't believe in them. This is a basic principle of successful marketing. Ultimately, your goal is to be authentic in how you present yourself (matching how you feel to the impression you give).

The Solar Plexus of the body is the center where you process emotion. It's from here you stake a claim to your place in the real world. Our emotions transmit our deepest expression; so, when you're going through any kind of transition, purifying on any level will greatly improve your condition.

44

Joy, Freshness, New Beginning, Expression, Gentleness, Beauty

A season of new expression is upon you! You can feel it in the wind, as it brushes behind the back of your neck, and the Sun, as it activates the sensation of movement in your body. Now you are ready and supported, in all ways, to do what may have felt like a risk at any other time.

What appears to be existing precariously can sometimes just be waiting for the right exposure to the elements to augment its maximum growth. Now is the time to embrace the power that gentleness inspires. Have confidence and take deliberate action; this will garner the universal support that is your birthright.

45

Harmony, Divine Relationship, Cooperation, Joy, Power, Group Dynamics, Patience

Synergy is the divine cooperative relationship between two or more beings, energies, or substances whose combined effect is far greater than any one of them alone. Synergy can be received as obvious or unseen help from sources known or unknown. Welcoming synergy into your life today acknowledges a higher standard of self-confidence, support, and resources—which are now yours.

Your willingness to move out of hibernation or isolation at this time will make a huge impact on all things in your life. Learning how to work in group dynamics is a skill set that must be practiced—patience, perseverance, and cooperation are the key dynamics at work right now in the current situation. How can you make peace?

One strand of thread holds tight, two strands bind securely, but three strands working together—fasten like no other and cannot be easily broken. *Ecclesiastes; 4:12*

46

Intuition, Apparition, Essence, Spiritual Force, Telepathy

The natural world brings us the whoosh of the wind, the grittiness of earth, the heat of fire, and the cool smooth sensation of water; but at any given time, we're privy to information that comes from everywhere around us. It's the third eye energy center—our internal voice of clairaudience, clairvoyance, and clairsentience—that receives spiritual details before we see, hear, or feel them in the physical realm.

At this time on the planet, we're cultivating our telepathy as a natural response to the Earth's changes and continuing spiritual shift. This shift moves us from a victimized perspective and hypervigilance, into an empowered telepathic state where we can consciously receive all the information we need when we need it.

When the Third Eye card chooses you, you've arrived at a profoundly important fork in the road. You can now decide to be accountable for all the details of your life: fortunate, unfortunate, or indifferent.

47

Communication, Expression, Translation, Feelings, Interpretation, Awareness

The way we communicate and the things we say have a lasting impact on ourselves and others and cannot be erased except with deliberate intent and shift to a new idea. Often our environment and the energy of others can have a subtle impact on us that we may not be aware of.

Pay attention to the words you choose and the tone you use; they can give you an indication of how your world is affecting you—it is where the things you are unconsciously picking up from your surroundings will reveal themselves.

Are your words charged with emotional pain, gratitude, or love? Are those your feelings? Do the chosen words suit what you wish to communicate exactly? Your current situation is asking you take stock of the way you speak to yourself and others. And the subtle effects of your impact, or others impact on you. Right now, honesty, awareness, and gratitude is your goal in the current situation.

48

Lovers, Romance, Sexuality, Intermingle, Connection, Intersection

Love's first connection with a partner is deliciously profound but ultimately fleeting. Romantic sexuality offers an opportunity to cultivate unspoken understanding, but it's the job of each partner to seize the opportunity. Connecting with others (ideologically, emotionally, spiritually, or physically) doesn't guarantee agreement. However, it can give a deeper understanding of one another—promoting love, compassion, and forgiveness.

Choosing this card today augurs the need for some form of unification relating to your current situation. Allow yourself to meditate on your heart's desire and what it means if it were to be fulfilled. Remember, relationships with others are the way we learn compassion for ourselves.

49

Awareness, Perspective, Vantage, Synergy, Oneness, Future, History, Grief

The Visionary card represents the opportunity to transform and expand how you see the world. Your current perspective comes from how you interpret your experiences and envision yourself. To become a visionary you must practice the universal flow of change. Surrendering to flow is a skill set that's cultivated. It takes practice to be calm and have awareness—simultaneously.

What is happening right now that you need to picture differently? What do you feel is your biggest obstacle to getting to another vantage? Being a visionary requires that you're able to take into consideration the needs of others in addition to your own—passing through phases of empathy and grief—which are the rite of passage. Let yourself grieve the loss of one image of success in order to align with success itself.

50

Struggle, Conflict Resolution, Control, Discipline, Overcome, Train, Courage

At the heart of every warrior is a cause they struggle to resolve. Once dealt with, another will appear—that is the way of the warrior. Discipline, control, and training are the benchmarks of the warrior's path. What is the best way to resolve the current situation? Does it require skills you possess, or is training necessary? What will it take to complete the task at hand?

This card heralds a time when you can find the solutions you seek. However, recognize that your true struggle is the process of finding the inner answers needed to quell or transform the outer conflict. No matter what, once in battle, a warrior never quits. However, there is no shame in quitting the path of the warrior.

51

Adapt, Emotion, Endurance, Fortitude, Expression, Continual Movement

Water is the most powerful of the five sacred elements. It can be slowed for a time but never stopped. Eventually, it will wear down even the tallest of mountains. It has few enemies and will adapt its ways with Fire to become steam. If Water is in your cards today, you're being asked to stay with the program. Don't give up!

Water may not be able to see every obstacle in advance, but it relishes the opportunity to be fully what it is—flexible. This is the time to embrace all your quirky unique ways and surrender to the magic that occurs when they are used synergistically in all you do.

52

Frozen, Rest, Hibernation, Possibilities, Prime, Trust, Security

What happens in the primary moments of any new cycle will be indicative of the rest of it. Trusting that initial phase sets a pace and a flow forward that allows for the most harmonious path possible toward the ordained accomplishment. A period of rest, repose, and reflection creates the space needed for all aspects of the self to align one's internal environment with one's external circumstances.

Receiving this card brings to your attention the need for solidarity and the importance of a plan when moving forward with the current situation or perspective. Resting at this time is not laziness; it's honoring the deepest call of the self to unify and consolidate, in preparation to begin again.

MEET THE AUTHORS

Justine Serebrin is a transformational channel, an intuitive artist, and the owner of the nationally praised Earth Altar Studio in Eagle Rock, California. Her career began as an artist, and shortly after channeling the art pieces that make up the RAINBOW WARRIOR ACTIVATION DECK, she envisioned offering her art to individuals to activate their own self-healing and embrace their most powerful selves through stunning permanent or temporary custom tattoo designs. She began using the cards as an oracle for the intuitive tattoo ritual that reveals the highest intentions and purpose of a tattoo's symbolism. Now, people come from all over the globe to have this transformational intuitive tattoo experience.

www.EarthAltarStudio.com

Tracee Dunblazier, GC-C, is a spiritual empath, shaman, and author of the critically acclaimed and award-winning *Demon Slayer's Handbook Series*. As a multi-sensitive, Tracee's blend of intuitive information combined with the use of different modalities has afforded thousands of people the opportunity to achieve deep healing and to create the success and peace they seek in their daily lives. Her compassionate, humorous, down-to-earth style empowers clients and readers to address difficult topics with courage, clarity, and joy. Tracee is consistently called upon by the media to provide expert commentary on spirituality, energy dynamics, and relationships.

www.TraceeDunblazier.com

BOOKS BY TRACEE

THE DEMON SLAYER'S HANDBOOK SERIES

"Tracee Dunblazier is answering a need that those afflicted by negative entities are desperately seeking… we think that any reader who is in need of assistance of slaying one's personal demons—or who wishes to help others slay theirs—will find this series invaluable."

Brad and Sherry Steiger
—*Authors of over 250 metaphysical titles*

Heal Your Soul History: Activate the True Power of Your Shadow will change how you look at your life and the lives of others from now on. Every page of this national award-winning 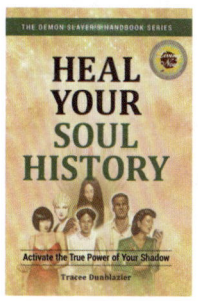 book will take you on a soul excavation, helping you to cultivate spiritual awareness and fostering the opportunity to resolve deep-seated life patterns that shape your everyday relationships. Learn the spiritual effects of post-traumatic stress, depression, and anxiety: what they mean to you and what to do about them. Be empowered by a living knowledge of your spirit and the way the universe works, while discovering the magnitude of your power in any situation. Most of all, understand the spiritual imprints of your unique soul and how they're impacting your life today.

"An inspirational guide to using a soul's long history to combat present-day negative forces."

Kirkus Reviews

"The book is for everyone who is trying to find a new perspective on the mysteries of life, and particularly for people who find human nature fascinating. **5 STARS!**"

SeriousReading.com

In, **Master Your Inner World: Embrace Your Power with Joy**, Tracee covers many relevant topics such as: spirit guides and other dimensional entities, tools for healing, the spiritual purpose of anger, grief, and depression and how to transform strong emotions. You'll receive a new framework for healing from the soul to the body in a way that adjusts your perspective of the underworld and shows you the magnitude of your power in any situation.

"An encouraging playbook for would-be demon-slayers."

Kirkus Reviews

"…Whether you start off with an open or closed mind, are at rush or at peace, reading with a light or heavy heart, Tracee's book will always offer the direction you need… **5 STARS!**"

SeriousReading.com